To my ancestors. For my future children.

"Walking, I am listening to a deeper way. Suddenly all my ancestors are behind me. Be still, they say. Watch and listen. You are the result of the love of thousands,"
—Linda Hogan

Minneapolis, MN 55455
www.leadtolove.com

No part of this publication may be reproduced or transmitted by any means without written permission of the publisher. For information regarding permission, contact the publisher (kristi@kristikremers.com).

Text and illustrations copyright © 2015 by Kristi L. Kremers.

All rights reserved. Published by Lead to Love Publishing.

ISBN-13: 978-1503053533
ISBN-10: 1503053539

WHO IS A LEADER?

A mindful approach for family & classroom discussions

KRISTI L. KREMERS

A leader is a person with dreams

I HAVE A DREAM

who can inspire people in the direction of a new future

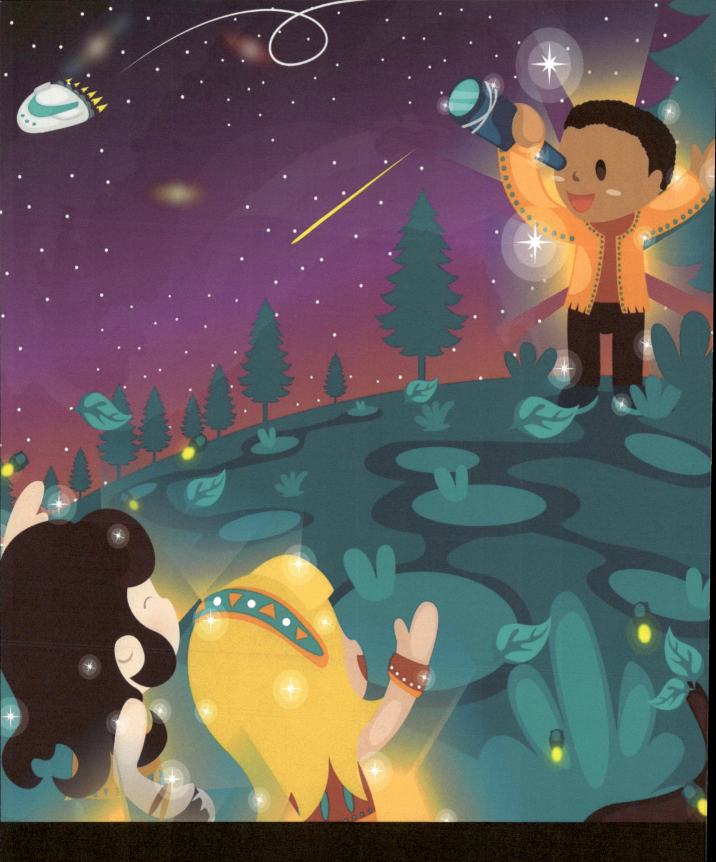
A leader looks at the universe outside

and also knows that we are made
of stars on the inside

A leader looks inside first

And makes decisions from their heart's compass

A leader takes care of themselves

And is invested in the well-being of their team

And doesn't leave them behind

A leader creates a culture

where people can be happy, successful and kind

where everyone feels safe,
honored and respected

A leader creates an environment

that brings out the best in others

whether they succeed or fail

A leader can be a Mom or a Dad

you will be a leader, too

Always follow your heart's compass

and even if no one joins you

"The ultimate measure of a man is not where he stands in moments of comfort and convenience, but where he stands at times of challenge and controversy."
-Dr. Martin Luther King, Jr.

LEADER PROFILES

Darkness does not drive out darkness; only light can do that. Hate cannot drive out hate; only love can do that.

Spread love everywhere you go. Let no one ever come to you without leaving happier.

We are all connected. To each other, biologically. To the earth, chemically. To the rest of the universe, atomically.

Dr. Martin Luther King Jr.

Dr. Martin Luther King, Jr. was a famous American civil rights leader and Baptist minister who promoted non-violent activism.

Questions for discussion: What are non-violent and violent forms of leadership? How did Martin Luther King Jr. use non-violence? How did his work change the history of race relations in the United States?

Mother Teresa

Mother Teresa was a Catholic nun from Kosovo. She spent most of her life in India where she developed soup kitchens, orphanages, schools and many services for the sick. She was dedicated to serving the poorest of the poor.

Question for discussion: How does/can our family serve others in need?

Dr. Neil deGrasse Tyson

Dr. Neil deGrasse Tyson is a famous astrophysicist, cosmologist and author. He is known for taking complex ideas and being able to communicate them in a way that connects with his audience.

Questions for discussion: Why is communication an important part of leadership? How do we know if communication (a) has occurred, and (b) it was successful?

FAMILY DISCUSSION GUIDE

Questions for Parents, Grandparents, and Other Wisdom Keepers: Talking About Leadership

1. How do you define leadership? What are the qualities of leaders you most admire?
2. What's your earliest memory of making a decision that required leadership? Did you make the right decision? Why or why not?
3. What did your parents teach you about what it means to be a leader?
4. What values were most important to your family when you were growing up?
5. Looking back at all of your ancestors, who is a family member that has inspired you most? Why?
6. What is the one leadership moment you are most proud of?
7. What is one that you wish you had handled differently?
8. Who are your favorite historical leaders? Why?
9. Who are your favorite leaders today? What qualities do they have that you wish to emulate?
10. What does the word integrity mean to you?

"Teaching kids to count is fine, but teaching them what counts is best."—Bob Talbert

QUESTIONS FOR CHILDREN

Talking About Leadership

1. How would you define what leadership is? What makes a good leader?
2. Who are your favorite leaders? Why?
3. When do you feel the most loved? How do you show your love to others?
4. If you have a conflict with a friend, what is the best way to resolve it?
5. What does it mean to be a leader in this family?
6. How do you create possibilities where everyone can win?
7. Who are your favorite friends? Why do you like them?
8. What are some of your qualities that make you a good friend to others?

Talking About Well-Being

1. When do you feel your best?
2. What does it mean to be healthy?
3. How do you take care of your health? Why is this important for a leader?
4. When you're angry or upset, what do you need? What makes you feel better? How do you help others who are angry or upset?

"Children are the living messengers we send to a time we will not see,"—Neil Postman

CLASSROOM DISCUSSION GUIDE

Questions (these can also be used as journal prompts):

1. Have your class brainstorm all the traits and behaviors of leaders. Define the difference between traits and behaviors. Give your students enough time to brainstorm first on their own (so introverts have time to process their ideas) and then bring the class together to create a mind map with all of the different characteristics of leaders.

2. *Journal Activity:* What are your top leadership traits and behaviors? When are you a leader at home or at school? Where can you improve your leadership?

3. What makes a vision inspirational?

4. Why is taking care of your own personal well-being an important aspect of being a good leader?

5. *Journal Activity:* What leader most inspires you? Why?

6. Talk about the leadership styles of Neil deGrasse Tyson, Oprah Winfrey, Martin Luther King, Jr., and/or Mother Teresa. What was their style of leadership? What makes them good leaders? What are the lessons that can be learned from their mistakes?

7. What's a "whistleblower"? When are there times a leader must make an unpopular decision?

For more activities and questions, visit: www.leadtolove.com

KRISTI L. KREMERS has been teaching at colleges and universities for the past decade. Her primary research interests include: emotional intelligence, ethics, neuroleadership, applied mindfulness in leadership, and how organizations can adapt an anthropological approach to creating culture and community.

In developing *Lead to Love*, it is her wish to create tools and resources for families and teachers to instill both a love for leadership, and a mindset to lead *with* love in children.

Visit Kristi's website: www.kristikremers.com
Author photo by the ultra-talented Tegan Jae: www.teganjae.com

Lead to love

We publish children's books with heart

A Leader Has Values: Active Learning Strategies for Engaging Family & Classroom Discussions
Paperback List Price: $15.99
Digital Copy: $4.99

BeeYOUtiful: A Storybook and Mindfulness Activity Guide
Paperback List Price: $15.99
Digital copy: FREE on www.leadtolove.com

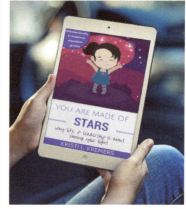

You Are Made of Stars: Why Life & Leadership is About Shining Your Light
Paperback List Price: $12.99
Digital Copy: $4.99

Who Is A Leader? A Mindful Approach for Family & Classroom Discussions
Paperback List Price: $12.99
Digital Copy: $4.99

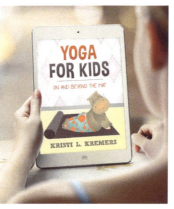

Yoga for Kids: On & Beyond the Mat
Paperback List Price: $13.99
Digital Copy: $4.99
Featured in Yoga Journal magazine

for more activities, and resources
visit our website
www.leadtolove.com

WWW.LEADTOLOVE.COM

CPSIA information can be obtained
at www.ICGtesting.com
Printed in the USA
LVHW070019170819
628028LV00023B/509/P